Greater Than a Tourist Book Series
Reviews from Readers

I think the series is wonderful and beneficial for tourists to get information before visiting the city.

-Seckin Zumbul, Izmir Turkey

I am a world traveler who has read many trip guides but this one really made a difference for me. I would call it a heartfelt creation of a local guide expert instead of just a guide.

-Susy, Isla Holbox, Mexico

New to the area like me, this is a must have!

-Joe, Bloomington, USA

This is a good series that gets down to it when looking for things to do at your destination without having to read a novel for just a few ideas.

-Rachel, Monterey, USA

Good information to have to plan my trip to this destination.

-Pennie Farrell, Mexico

Great ideas for a port day.

-Mary Martin USA

Aptly titled, you won't just be a tourist after reading this book. You'll be greater than a tourist!

-Alan Warner, Grand Rapids, USA

Even though I only have three days to spend in San Miguel in an upcoming visit, I will use the author's suggestions to guide some of my time there. An easy read - with chapters named to guide me in directions I want to go.

 -Robert Catapano, USA

Great insights from a local perspective! Useful information and a very good value!

 -Sarah, USA

This series provides an in-depth experience through the eyes of a local. Reading these series will help you to travel the city in with confidence and it'll make your journey a unique one.

-Andrew Teoh, Ipoh, Malaysia

GREATER THAN A TOURIST- DUBLIN IRELAND

50 Travel Tips from a Local

Sarah Whelan

First Edition

Cover designed by: https://pixabay.com/photos/bridge-dublin-ireland-eire-city-230311/

Cover Image: Ivana Stamenkovic

Image 1: https://en.wikipedia.org/wiki/File:Dublin_-_Father_Mathew_Bridge_-_110508_182542.jpg Barcex / CC BY-SA (https://creativecommons.org/licenses/by-sa/3.0)

Image 2: https://en.wikipedia.org/wiki/File:The_Dubhlinn_Gardens_Dublin_Castle_01.JPG J.-H. Janßen / CC BY-SA (https://creativecommons.org/licenses/by-sa/3.0)

Image 3: https://en.wikipedia.org/wiki/File:HENRIETTA_STREET_-_DUBLIN_(402556531).jpg William Murphy from Dublin, Ireland / CC BY-SA (https://creativecommons.org/licenses/by-sa/2.0)

Image 4: https://en.wikipedia.org/wiki/File:Dublin_City_Council_Civic_Offices.JPG YvonneM / CC BY-SA (https://creativecommons.org/licenses/by-sa/3.0)

CZYK Publishing Since 2011.
Greater Than a Tourist

Lock Haven, PA
All rights reserved.

ISBN: 9798632542883

>TOURIST

50 TRAVEL TIPS FROM A LOCAL

BOOK DESCRIPTION

With travel tips and culture in our guidebooks written by a local author, it is never too late to visit Dublin. Greater Than a Tourist - Dublin by Author Sarah Whelan offers the inside scoop on Dublin's fair city. Most travel books tell you how to travel like a tourist. Although there is nothing wrong with that, as part of the 'Greater Than a Tourist' series, this book will give you candid travel tips from someone who has lived at your next travel destination. This guide book will not tell you exact addresses or store hours but instead gives you knowledge that you may not find in other smaller print travel books. Experience cultural, culinary delights, and attractions with the guidance of a Local. Slow down and get to know the people with this invaluable guide. By the time you finish this book, you will be eager and prepared to discover new activities at your next travel destination.

Inside this travel guide book you will find:

Visitor information from a Local
Tour ideas and inspiration
Save time with valuable guidebook information

Greater Than a Tourist- A Travel Guidebook with 50 Travel Tips from a Local. Slow down, stay in one place, and get to know the people and culture. By the time you finish this book, you will be eager and prepared to travel to your next destination.

OUR STORY

Traveling is a passion of the Greater than a Tourist book series creator. Lisa studied abroad in college, and for their honeymoon Lisa and her husband toured Europe. During her travels to Malta, an older man tried to give her some advice based on his own experience living on the island since he was a young boy. She was not sure if she should talk to the stranger but was interested in his advice. When traveling to some places she was wary to talk to locals because she was afraid that they weren't being genuine. Through her travels, Lisa learned how much locals had to share with tourists. Lisa created the Greater Than a Tourist book series to help connect people with locals. A topic that locals are very passionate about sharing.

TABLE OF CONTENTS

11. Try some of the best coffee and bottomless brunch spots in town
12. Grab a cocktail at a secret cocktail bar
13. For a more casual night out, play some board games and drink craft beers

Go on the best tours that Dublin has to offer
14. Learn to shout like a real Viking
15. Take part in a spooky Ghost Bus tour… if you dare!
16. Learn how to pour the perfect pint
17. Take a tour of the famous Jameson Distillery
18. Got a sweet tooth? Go on a tour of a real chocolate factory
19. Take a 1916 walking tour
20. For something much more light-hearted, learn about the history of Irish Leprechauns
21. Take a fun workshop
22. Discover your Irish roots
23. Take your knowledge of whiskey up a notch
24. Visit the historic Kilmainham Gaol
25. Take a trip to Phoenix Park and stroll around the Zoo
26. Peek at the bullet holes from the 1916 Rising at the GPO
27. Stroll the galleries and grounds of IMMA

DEDICATION

This book is dedicated to my mam Dee, and all the wonderful Irish mammies.

ABOUT THE AUTHOR

Sarah is a proud Irish woman who lives in north Dublin. She loves to immerse herself in art, theatre, sport and the rich culture that Ireland has to offer. She also enjoys long walks followed by a cold creamy pint of Guinness, preferably beside an open fire.

HOW TO USE THIS BOOK

The *Greater Than a Tourist* book series was written by someone who has lived in an area for over three months. The goal of this book is to help travelers either dream or experience different locations by providing opinions from a local. The author has made suggestions based on their own experiences. Please check before traveling to the area in case the suggested places are unavailable.

Travel Advisories: As a first step in planning any trip abroad, check the Travel Advisories for your intended destination.
https://travel.state.gov/content/travel/en/traveladvisories/traveladvisories.html

FROM THE PUBLISHER

Traveling can be one of the most important parts of a person's life. The anticipation and memories that you have are some of the best. As a publisher of the Greater Than a Tourist, as well as the popular *50 Things to Know* book series, we strive to help you learn about new places, spark your imagination, and inspire you. Wherever you are and whatever you do I wish you safe, fun, and inspiring travel.

Lisa Rusczyk Ed. D.
CZYK Publishing

WELCOME TO
> TOURIST

Father Mathew Bridge, also known as Dublin Bridge

The Dubhlinn Gardens with Dublin Castle in the background,
Dublin, Ireland.

Henrietta Street, developed in the 1720s is the earliest Georgian street in Dublin.

Civic Offices of Dublin City Council

*"Live life with no excuses, travel
with no regret"*

– Oscar Wilde.

I have lived in Dublin city for five years. I grew up in a town called Newbridge on the border of Dublin. I knew one day I would live in the buzz and bustle of this fantastic city. Dublin is world famous for many reasons; its art, poetry, music, storytelling, theatre – but also for the "craic", which is an Irish word for fun or enjoyment. Irish people love the craic. In fact, "What's the craic?" is our favourite and most commonly used greeting, loosely meaning "Where is the fun?"

As you walk through the streets of Dublin, you will find people of all ages and nationalities looking for the craic. That may be in a crowded pub singing songs and drinking pints, walking along the coast on a sunny day eating ice-cream while looking out at the blue Irish Sea, or sitting in a café with a coffee and chatting with your friends. The craic is here, and ready to be had! This book is all about how to have the most craic possible on your trip to Dublin, written from the heart of someone who loves the city, and wants the rest of the world to love it too.

What to eat in Dublin's fair city

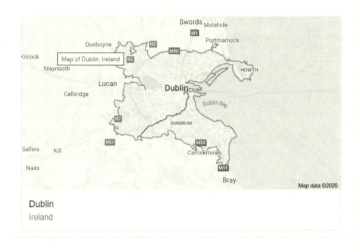

Dublin
Ireland

Dublin Climate

	High	Low
January	46	35
February	47	36
March	51	37
April	55	39
May	60	43
June	65	48
July	68	52
August	67	52
September	63	48
October	57	44
November	51	39
December	47	37

GreaterThanaTourist.com

Temperatures are in Fahrenheit degrees.
Source: NOAA

1. SAMPLE TRADITIONAL IRISH FOOD

Dublin is full to the brim of restaurants, cafés, diners and buffets of all cuisines. There isn't a chance of you going hungry on your trip. However, if you want a traditional Irish meal, you should head to a pub as opposed to a restaurant, where traditional food is more likely to be on the menu. There are many of these pubs in the city centre and on the outskirts. Meals in Irish pubs are usually inexpensive, the portions are generous, and you can partner your dinner with a pint of Guinness or finish off with an Irish coffee. In the morning time, I would highly recommend a full Irish breakfast, complete with Irish blood pudding and local pork sausages. In the evening, a traditional Irish stew made with potatoes and home-grown vegetables, lamb or beef will warm you up after a long day of strolling the city.

2. STROLL THE ICONIC COBBLES AND GRAB A QUICK LUNCH IN TEMPLE BAR

If you've devoured your tasty Irish breakfast and you're not hungry enough for a big hearty bowl of Irish stew just yet, you can grab a quick snack or a coffee in the bustling Temple Bar area of the city. Temple Bar is one of the most historic areas of the city dating back as far as the 16th century. These days, it is more well-known among locals as a tourist trap. As a rule of thumb, I would try to spend as little time in the restaurants and bars of Temple Bar as possible, as these are unfortunately over-priced. However, there are so many free art galleries, vintage thrift shops and music venues in Temple Bar, that you can take a load off at one of the many quaint independent cafés in the area, where a coffee and a pastry or sandwich are inexpensive and you can people-watch from a window seat at your leisure.

3. TRY SOME INTERNATIONAL CUISINE ON CAPEL STREET

Dubliners love to meet friends for lunch and dinner, and as a nation, we have varied tastes. If Irish cuisine isn't your thing, there are streets full of Vietnamese, Japanese, Chinese, Indian and Thai restaurants open seven days a week just a short walk from the city centre. Capel street is one such street, where you can grab a delicious steamy bowl of pho or a plate of fresh sushi. Capel street also boasts several bars, pubs, cafés and all-you-can-eat buffets. No matter what your palate, you are bound to find something tasty to keep you going throughout the day. I highly recommend taking a stroll down Capel street when you are finished your lunch and browsing in some of the second-hand antique shops. Who knows what treasures you might find there?

4. FANCY SOMETHING A LITTLE MORE FORMAL? CHECK OUT THE WORLD-RENOWNED RESTAURANTS ON THE SOUTH SIDE OF THE CITY

Dublin city centre is full of four- and five-star restaurants that are guaranteed to be a hit. Many of these fine-dining locations are on the South side of the city, on Dawson Street, Camden Street and off the famous Grafton Street. The South side of Dublin is well-known for having more up-scale eateries and bars than the North side. These restaurants can be quite busy, so booking a table well ahead of time is recommended. There are many different cuisines to choose from, including American steak houses, French, Italian or classic fine dining. You can also check the menus online before you book in case anyone in your party has any dietary requirements or preferences. As a head's up, it is customary to tip your wait staff at these restaurants, although it is not mandatory like it is in some other countries. You can usually tip using your credit or debit card at the end of your meal, or you can tip staff using cash. Again, it's not essential to tip, however if your service has been great throughout your meal, it can be nice to give back to the wait staff.

5. GET OUT OF THE CITY CENTRE AND DISCOVER SOME REAL GEMS

Many tourists stick to the city centre when they visit Dublin, but there are hundreds of pubs, bars and restaurants a short journey outside of the centre that are an excellent choice for dinner or after-dinner cocktails. The Luas is the tram that travels through the city and it is a quick and inexpensive way of getting to the suburbs, away from the craziness of the city centre. Luas stops are dotted all around the city, including O'Connell Street and Dawson Street. The tram can take you to areas like Ranelagh, Rathmines and Phibsboro, where there are even more options for food and drink, and can be less crowded than the city. Ranelagh is on the south side and is well known for being full of delicious casual evening spots, as well as some classy fine dining options. There are also plenty of places in Ranelagh that offer bottomless brunches and healthy options during the day. At night-time, Ranelagh is buzzing with young professionals and students meeting up for drinks in the many bars and pubs. This makes the small suburb a great choice to start your evening before venturing into the city centre to sample its nightlife. Phibsboro is based on the north side of the city and is also full of fantastic bars and restaurants, some of which are unknown to even the most seasoned Dublin diner. There are Irish cafés and restaurants that have been around for generations and are steeping in history on the north side. Hedigans (AKA the Brian Ború) in Phibsboro is one such location, which has been serving food and drinks for two hundred years! Don't be afraid to strike up a conversation with some of the people you meet at these north side restaurants and bars to learn more about the history and hear their stories. Dubliners love to tell a good tale!

6. VEGETARIAN? NO PROBLEM!

Dublin is very modern and has tons of options to cater for pescatarians, vegetarians and vegans alike. Almost every restaurant you venture into will have a wealth of veggie options on their menu. There are also plenty of falafel and vegan restaurants to choose from in the city centre. Umi Falafel is a fast food falafel joint that makes great sandwiches and mezze plates. Their deep-fried halloumi sticks are my favourite weekend treat! Cornucopia on Wicklow Street also serves up a wide variety of delicious vegetarian and vegan dishes, such as veggie lasagnes and moussakas, that are inexpensive and huge in portion.

WHAT TO DRINK AND WHERE

7. EXPERIENCE THE PROPER PINT OF GUINNESS

Guinness is the traditional beer of Ireland. It is a dark dry stout and has become world famous. Guinness originated in the brewery of Arthur Guinness at St. James's Gate in 1759. If you venture to the Guinness Store House, you will learn all about the components of the perfect pint, fondly known by Dubliners as "the black stuff" or in areas outside of Dublin "a pint of plain". However, even if you don't visit the Storehouse you will still have plenty of opportunities to sample as many pints of the black stuff as you can handle. Wherever you may be in Dublin, you are only a stone's throw away from a pub, each one competing with the next for the finest pint of Guinness. The best pints are usually found in the older and more established pubs of Dublin. The Gravediggers Pub in Glasnevin is often celebrated as the number one pub in Dublin for pints of Guinness and is also seeping in Irish history. The pub got its unusual name as it is built into the wall of the historic Glasnevin cemetery and is where gravediggers would come to drink pints after a hard day's work. The décor hasn't changed much since the 1800s when the pub first opened its doors, and cash is the only form of payment accepted here. A trip to Gravediggers is essential when looking for the perfect pint of Guinness, however if stout isn't to your taste, you also have a wide range of wines, shorts and hot food to choose from. Check out the towers along the walls of the cemetery outside the Gravediggers pub. This is where guards would lookout for grave robbing, which was a lucrative business back in the 1800s. The robbers weren't just searching for jewellery or gold, they would dig up the corpses to sell to scientists for medical research for large rewards. Thankfully, this morbid practise is long out of date!

8. ROOFTOP BARS ARE A GREAT OPTION TO RELAX WITH VIEWS OF THE CITY

When you have spent all day walking the many streets of Dublin, it can be nice to take stock of the city from one of the stylish rooftop bars. Most of these rooftop getaways are located on the south side and have a wide selection of drinks and small bites to eat. They can be busy, so get in early to catch a glimpse of the sun going down over the Dublin horizon. The Marker Hotel in Grand Canal Dock has a modern rooftop bar with a fabulous view of the bustling Docklands, which can be an ideal romantic date night for a couple. If you're looking for somewhere even more central, Sophie's Bar in the Dean Hotel on Harcourt Street has a vast array of cocktails and a fabulous view of the Dublin skyline. You can then venture into one of the many hopping nightclubs on offer on Harcourt Street.

9. SEE WHY DUBLIN IS A MUSIC LOVER'S DREAM

Irish people love music of all genres. That's why as you're rambling the streets, you are bound to catch a hint of music coming from pubs, shops, restaurants and venues. There are a huge number of live music venues in the city centre. Whelan's on Wexford Street is one of the most popular music locations in the city, with some of the world's best-known acts playing here to an intimate audience. The acoustics are often applauded as being some of the best in the world. There is always some form of live band playing here in the evening, so you are guaranteed to be entertained while you sip your pint. The most popular music genre in Dublin among the younger generation is house and dance music. There are plenty of clubs in the city centre dedicated to dancing into the early hours of the morning, including The Button Factory and Opium, which are both based on the south side, and the Bernard Shaw based on the north side. If you are a techno music fan and fancy dancing the night away at a gig, you can check out Index and Jam Park, both on the north side of the city. These nightclubs host international and Irish techno DJs every weekend. If rock music is more your scene, you can check out Fibber Magees which is right on the Quays, making it very accessible to all rock-lovers. For pop music listeners, there are a plethora of nightclubs dedicated to pop music along the famous Harcourt Street, such as the infamous Coppers Nightclub, and on Dawson Street, like the sleek and stylish Café en Seine. Both have a live DJ to entertain the busy crowds each weekend. There really is a music option for everyone. You may have to pay an entry fee to these clubs, which is usually inexpensive, but worth bearing in mind when deciding which venue to spend your evening.

10. SAMPLE TRADITIONAL IRISH MUSIC

Traditional Irish music is more commonly found on the West and in the South of the country, however if you are on the hunt for some famous traditional Irish music in Dublin, you will be pleasantly surprised to find plenty of Irish music spots in the city centre and the surrounding areas. The Cobblestone, which is based in Smithfield and calls itself "A drinking pub with a music problem" is one such pub where real traditional Irish music can be heard. The Mulligan family who own the pub have been playing traditional Irish music for five generations and have a deep respect for Irish music and culture. Another great venue for authentic Irish music is Devitts Pub on Camden Street, where trad sessions are held every day, seven days a week. As traditional Irish music is slowly becoming a thing of the past, Irish people love to share their native musical history with visitors. Don't be afraid to chat to some of the travelling trad performers once they have finished playing - they're usually some of the most interesting people in the city and have plenty of stories to tell!

11. TRY SOME OF THE BEST COFFEE AND BOTTOMLESS BRUNCH SPOTS IN TOWN

In Dublin, we love our independent coffee brewers, bakeries and cafés, and as such we enjoy the opportunity to recommend them to coming visitors. There are so many fantastic independent businesses to try in Dublin that it would be impossible to name them all. One stand-out would be Two Boys Brew based in Phibsboro, with some of the best coffee and tasty brunch options that Dublin has to offer. The owners and staff are very welcoming and friendly, and the café is a huge hit with locals on the north side. At weekends, there is usually a queue stretching as far as Croke Park patiently waiting to enjoy a delicious breakfast, but on weekdays, you will be able to grab a seat with no problem. Just up the road from Two Boys Brew is Bang Bang, another curious Irish-owned café that boasts a small vintage shop and a host of old books and relics to flick through while you enjoy a cup of delicious coffee. If you keep your eyes peeled while walking through the city centre you will spot more small brunch and coffee spots, especially along Camden Street and George's Street. Take shelter in the historic George's Arcade, which has been open since 1881 and watch the world go by from one of the café windows with a hot cup of tea or coffee. For something a little boozier, gather your pals for a bottomless brunch in the city centre. South William Street on the south side of the city is just a short walk from Grafton street and at weekends is packed with brunch diners at cafés such as Platform 61, where prosecco and mimosas are free flowing, and eggs are poached to perfection.

12. GRAB A COCKTAIL AT A SECRET COCKTAIL BAR

Hidden away in the bustle of Temple Bar is the exclusive Vintage Cocktail Club, a 1920s clandestine bar behind a secret doorway. You must ring the doorbell and wait to be admitted, like a time-warp back to the mysterious and exciting days of prohibition and speakeasies. The cocktails are second to none at the Vintage Cocktail Club, the menu is extensive, and the atmosphere is electric. They also serve delicious small plates in case you feel like a bite to accompany your cocktails. A night at the Vintage Cocktail Club can be expensive, but I highly recommend popping in for a cocktail (or two) to wrap up an evening in the city. There are other secretive bars in the city, such as The Hacienda Bar in Smithfield, a charming little wine bar where, again, you must ring the bell and wait to gain entry. From experience, large groups will not be permitted, however The Hacienda Bar is the perfect spot for a romantic glass of wine in one of their cosy nooks.

13. FOR A MORE CASUAL NIGHT OUT, PLAY SOME BOARD GAMES AND DRINK CRAFT BEERS

There are numerous hip pubs and bars in Dublin designed for small and large groups to hang out, drink delicious craft beers, eat pizza and play board games. Cassidy's is one such pub, located on Westmoreland Street, conveniently located right beside the Luas stop. Cassidy's is always buzzing with local students, professionals destressing after their workday and tourists from all over the world. There are three floors: jazz in the basement, a piano bar and a large open area on the ground floor. Established in 1856, Cassidy's also has a very interesting history. It was once the home of The Freeman's Journal, the oldest national newspaper in Ireland and the primary media supporter of the leaders of the 1916 Rising. Today, it is a bohemian meeting point for revellers to relax, enjoy games of Jenga and sample some of their delicious craft beers well into the night.

GO ON THE BEST TOURS THAT DUBLIN HAS TO OFFER

14. LEARN TO SHOUT LIKE A REAL VIKING

Everyone who visits Dublin will have seen or heard the battle cries of the Viking Splash Tour as it rumbles through the streets and the water, roaring and cheering as it goes along. This award-winning tour of the city is well-known for having passengers in peals of laughter throughout, while also imparting some of the city's Viking history. Beginning at St Stephen's Green, the tour trundles through the city's medieval landmarks on a bright yellow amphibious floating bus, while the notoriously hilarious tour guides give insights into the city's Viking roots. I cannot recommend the Viking Splash tour enough, especially for groups and families. It gives an entertaining and alternative method of viewing the city that gets every trainee Viking involved, guaranteed to put a smile on your face.

15. TAKE PART IN A SPOOKY GHOST BUS TOUR... IF YOU DARE!

The Ghost Bus tour starts after nightfall at College Green right beside Trinity College and is another excellent way of viewing the city - this time the city's more sinister side. The Irish love to tell stories, and ghost stories are no different. The Ghost Bus tour is the perfect way to hear some of the dark paranormal tales that have enchanted Dubliners for generations. You will explore some of the most haunted areas of Dublin, including a creepy vault hidden in Dublin castle and, of course, the haunted crypts at0. Glasnevin cemetery. The tour guides are all professional actors and are excellent at getting every passenger laughing…or crying! Be prepared for a couple of truly frightening moments while on the Ghost Bus - as well as some great craic!

16. LEARN HOW TO POUR THE PERFECT PINT

Not only is the visit to the world-famous Guinness Storehouse essential to understanding the components of the perfect pint of plain, it is also a great way to spend an afternoon. The view of Dublin's skyline from the Gravity Bar at the top of the storehouse is breath-taking. There are several specialty tours that you can take depending on how you feel on the day, including a more intimate experience with a beer specialist at the private Connoisseur Bar. You can even order a "STOUTie", which is a pint with your own face printed on the delicious creamy top! The Guinness Storehouse is Ireland's number one attraction and, as such, can be quite busy, so make sure to reserve your tickets online in advance.

17. TAKE A TOUR OF THE FAMOUS JAMESON DISTILLERY

If the history of our most famous Irish whiskey is more up your alley, you are in luck. Smithfield on the north inner city boasts the prominent Jameson

Distillery, which is over 200 years old. Here you can take a tour of the old distillery and learn all about the infamous Irish whiskey and its ancient brewing techniques - some of which are still being used in Jameson whiskey production today. Finish off the tour with a comparative whiskey tasting or a cocktail making class. You also get a delicious complimentary Jameson beverage at the end of the tour. A visit to this distillery would make a great start to a day of exploring the city. It is short, sweet and very accessible, with the Luas right on its doorstep.

18. GOT A SWEET TOOTH? GO ON A TOUR OF A REAL CHOCOLATE FACTORY

Butler's Chocolate Cafés can be found in many locations throughout Dublin, including the top of Grafton Street beside St Stephen's Green and the busy Henry Street. Their coffee is delightful, and the complimentary chocolates are a heavenly treat while exploring the city. If you have sampled a delicious Butler's coffee and chocolate combination and find yourself wanting more, then the Butler's Chocolate Tour is for you. The Butler's factory is based outside of the city centre and is easily accessible using Dublin Bus. The tour gives you an insight into the workings of a real chocolate factory, demonstrating how the chocolate is made and where the ingredients come from. The Chocolate Tour is great for families and groups with children. Each visitor gets to decorate and customize their own chocolates to take home - the perfect souvenir to commemorate a day learning about one of the world's favourite sweet treats!

19. TAKE A 1916 WALKING TOUR

As many people coming to Dublin to visit will know, Ireland has a long history of violence and rebellion. Ireland was ruled by Britain for centuries, until in 1916, Dublin was thrust into an era of revolution. A small band of insurrectionists declared Ireland to be a Republic, and the 1916 Easter Rising followed. Many important buildings within the city were strategically seized by Irish rebels during the Rising, including the GPO and a prominent factory. The British army retaliated, bringing gun-fire to the city's streets and many Irish people, rebels and civilians alike, lost their lives. The Irish revolution was ultimately successful, and today we have the leaders of the 1916 Rising to thank for their efforts. The 1916 Rising is encapsulated by the city of Dublin, and the perfect way to learn this fascinating story is by taking part in one of the many 1916 walking tours that are given by local guides. One of the best of these tours is the 1916 Rebellion Walking Tour, given by Irish historian Lorcan Collins. There are also several 1916 bus tours on offer if you prefer to view the historic sites in comfort, which may be a good option in case of rain. Whichever tour operator you decide is best for your group, learning about Dublin's defiant and revolutionary history will teach you a great deal about Irish people in general, for example, why were are so proud of our Republic and give you some background to the tenacity and patriotism of the local people.

20. FOR SOMETHING MUCH MORE LIGHT-HEARTED, LEARN ABOUT THE HISTORY OF IRISH LEPRECHAUNS

The Leprechaun Museum beside Jervis Shopping Centre is a tongue-in-cheek art centre that is great for families and groups with younger children to delve into the magical world of the leprechaun. Us Irish know that the world loves to hear leprechaun folklore and stories featuring other Irish mythical creatures, and what better way to honour them than with an immersive museum, complete with some great props for photo opportunities. This would be the perfect spot for an hour of laughs and jokes after lunch as the museum is right in the city centre, beside plenty of cafés and restaurants. There is a gift shop full of hilarious souvenirs to take home too.

21. TAKE A FUN WORKSHOP

Hidden away in Beggar's Bush, a short bus journey from the city centre, is the National Print Museum. The Print Museum runs two interactive tours a day on the art of letterpress printing, a tradition that has recently been added to the protected heritage list. If you want a more immersive experience, you can take a workshop in calligraphy, book binding, card-making and more. There are a host of fun children's events to look out for on the Print Museum website all year round and festive Christmas markets too. One thing about the National Print Museum that is unknown to many Dubliners, is that the original 1916 Proclamation, the document issued by the Irish Citizen Army during the 1916 Easter Rising to instate the Irish Republic, is on display at the Print Museum. The National Print Museum also has the machine that would have been used to create the Proclamation over a hundred years ago. This makes the Print Museum a fantastic penultimate visit for anyone interested in the history of the Irish Republic.

22. DISCOVER YOUR IRISH ROOTS

As many people will know, you can find Irish people in all corners of the globe. Many American, European and Australian visitors come to Ireland every year to connect the dots of their own heritage. The best place to do this is the sleek and modern Immigration Museum, based in the North Docks of the City, beside the Samuel Beckett bridge, in the vaults of CHQ. EPIC The Irish Immigration Museum offers a fully immersive experience, where visitors can understand the mobilisation of the island's native population through the centuries, moving from room to room of the museum. The Immigration Museum is conveniently located right beside the Famine Memorial. The Irish Potato Famine was the event that kicked off the huge displacement of millions of Irish people and changed that landscape of Ireland forever. You can find out more about your own Irish ancestry, the truth about the Irish famine and the difficulties facing global immigration of the past and present.

23. TAKE YOUR KNOWLEDGE OF WHISKEY UP A NOTCH

The Irish Whiskey Museum is located on College Green beside Grafton Street, one of the busiest shopping districts in the city. The Irish Whiskey museum is independent of all distilleries and is an essential stop for whiskey-lovers around the world. The guides at the museum are second to none in their knowledge of the 2000-year history of whiskey. There are four rooms, each designed around a period of Ireland's past, where the guides will take you on a journey of Irish whiskey through the ages. At the end of the tour you will have the chance to become a true whiskey connoisseur. Irish whiskey can also be sampled at any of the bars and pubs in the city. Whether you prefer a Whiskey Sour or an Old Fashioned, there are plenty of options for enthusiasts. Speak to any of the mixologists at some of the bars on Dawson Street and they will be more than happy to try and impress you with their selection.

24. VISIT THE HISTORIC KILMAINHAM GAOL

Kilmainham Gaol (pronounced Jail) is the haunting former prison where the leaders of the Irish revolution were detained. It was operational between 1764 and 1924, where Irish rebels were held by the British Army, not only during the 1916 Rising, but during the many Irish rebellions beforehand. The Gaol is now a very popular attraction, visited frequently by Irish people and foreign tourists alike. The Gaol tour is guaranteed to leave an impression, especially the grounds where the firing squad executed Irish citizens who were deemed by the British Army to have connection to the rebellion. The Gaol gives an insight into the harsh reality of the lives of the revolutionary leaders and the lives of normal Irish citizens, many of whom met their end at the Kilmainham Gaol.

25. TAKE A TRIP TO PHOENIX PARK AND STROLL AROUND THE ZOO

Who doesn't love a trip to the zoo? Dublin Zoo is nestled on the grounds of the idyllic and well-kept Phoenix Park on the north side of the city. Phoenix Park is the largest park in Dublin and is a popular local spot among north side Dubliners for picnics, weekend fun-runs and dog walking. There are plenty of ice-cream vans during the summer and cafés serving delicious coffee and sandwiches if you would like to have a bite to eat before strolling through the famous Dublin Zoo. The Zoo has been open since 1831 and attracts over a million visitors a year. This is mainly due to its handy location within Phoenix Park and its reputation for being an immaculate zoo, with a focus on conservation and veterinary sciences.

26. PEEK AT THE BULLET HOLES FROM THE 1916 RISING AT THE GPO

The GPO stands for the General Post Office and is the headquarters for An Post, the Irish Postal Service. However, that is not why it attracts thousands of visitors each year. During the 1916 Easter Rising, rebels occupied the building on O'Connell Street and made it their headquarters. It is outside this famous building that Padraig Pearse read out the Proclamation of the Irish Republic. The building was destroyed in a fire in the course of the rebellion and the granite façade at the front still bears the marks of the historic gunfire. The GPO was rebuilt in 1929, and to this day is a symbol of Irish nationalism. Inside the GPO today is a museum called "GPO Witness History", which is dedicated to documenting this milestone.

Get a feel for Irish art and culture

27. STROLL THE GALLERIES AND GROUNDS OF IMMA

The Irish Museum of Modern Art hosts Ireland's contemporary art and photography and is a must-see for all culture enthusiasts visiting Dublin. Situated in Kilmainham just a short walk from Heuston Train Station, IMMA's admission is free and the building itself constructed on a beautiful 48 acres of land previously known as the Royal Hospital Kilmainham, a former 17th century hospital. Inside the Museum, the Visitor Engagement Team are extremely knowledgeable and provide 30-minute guided tours that are also free of charge. I highly recommend speaking with one of the team to learn more about the Irish contemporary art movements or pieces that catch your eye. They are more than happy to answer any questions as you wander through the galleries. When you have perused the general and the special art exhibitions, you can reflect in the picturesque meadows and formal gardens. Grab a cup of coffee in the café and chat with your fellow travellers about some of the installations you have seen or visit the gift shop and bring home an artistic souvenir.

28. WATCH A PLAY AT THE SMOCK ALLEY THEATRE

Ireland produced some of the best playwrights that the world has ever seen; Samuel Beckett, George Bernard Shaw, William Butler Yeats, Sean O'Casey – the list could go on and on! Today, theatre is still at the core of Irish culture and heritage. On any evening during the week, there will be a performance on one of the many stages throughout the city. The Smock Alley Theatre based on the Quays is my favourite theatre in Dublin. Built in 1662, the Smock Alley Theatre has a long and interesting history. It started as a playhouse known as the Royal Theatre. It then downgraded to a lowly whiskey warehouse, before transitioning to a Catholic Church for a time, and eventually becoming a theatre once more. The old bricks are some of the oldest ones laid in Dublin. It is now home to the best of Irish song, dance and creativity. The performances here are usually inexpensive and easy to book online. The focus of the Smock Alley Theatre is to support emerging Irish actors, producers, directors and playwrights. It is a hub for local and international theatre festivals, including Scene and Heard and the Fringe Festival. I highly recommend making an evening out of a visit to the Smock Alley. Grab a glass of wine before the performance and be entertained by some of the newest Irish theatre talent.

29. CATCH A FILM AT THE IRISH FILM INSTITUTE IN TEMPLE BAR

Temple Bar is jam-packed with free galleries, exhibitions and art installations. It is also home to the IFI, the Irish Film Institute, which is one of the busiest and most dynamic arts organisations in the country. The IFI shows the best of independent, Irish and international cinema and is the host of several Irish film festivals throughout the year, including the Virgin Media Dublin International Film Festival. The Institute holds many events, panel discussions and regularly shows material from their vast Irish moving-picture archives that stretch from 1897 Ireland to the present day. Pop into the IFI at lunchtime for a free film showing every Monday, Wednesday and Saturday, or book your tickets to see an internationally acclaimed movie any evening of the week using the IFI website.

30. LOSE YOURSELF IN THE NATIONAL GALLERY OF IRELAND

The National Gallery of Ireland is another gem based a short walk from the central shopping district of Grafton Street. Admission to the Gallery's massive general collection is free, which makes it a hit among art-loving Dubliners and travellers alike. The Gallery hosts the national collection of European art and many other temporary special collections throughout the year. There are over 16,000 pieces of art from famous Irish artists, including Jack B Yeats and James Barry, and world celebrated artists such as Caravaggio. With its huge collection and multiple exhibitions, you can easily get lost among the paintings, sculptures, photography and installations. I highly recommend starting your voyage through the gallery with a portable audio guide. It is also worth checking the National Gallery's website for more information on the temporary collections, as these are quite exclusive and could book up quickly.

31. WANDER THE GROUNDS OF DUBLIN CASTLE

Dublin Castle is conveniently based off Dame Street in the city centre. It was the seat   of the British Government's administration in Ireland until 1922. The Castle dates back as far as the 13th century on the site of a Viking settlement. The Castle is sometimes used for State functions, otherwise it is fully open to the public. Tours of the Castle are inexpensive, although you are free to walk the grounds and explore on your own with no charge. Visiting Dublin Castle is a great way to spend a half an hour in between adventures as it is so central. It is also a stone's throw away from the Dublinia tourist centre, which is worth a venture if you are interested in learning even more about the Vikings in Ireland.

32. READ THE BOOK OF KELLS AT TRINITY COLLEGE

Many people around the world will know of the most famous medieval manuscript, the Book of Kells. However, not many people will get the opportunity to see it. The Book of Kells is an ancient 9th century manuscript that documents the four Gospels. It is on display all year round at the historic Trinity College of Dublin, based on College Green in the Old Library, an 18th century building that many people will recognise from photos as the inspiration behind the Hogwarts Library in the Harry Potter sequel. The Book of Kells exhibition will give you all the information you need on the long and fascinating history of the text, but the Book itself is also a sight to behold. Its intricate and lavish decoration is stunning to the eye. If you don't want to take a look at the historic book, you are free to wander the grounds of Trinity College free of charge, a university that has been open since 1592 and produced countless Irish scholars. The lush grounds of Trinity College are a great place to unwind after waiting in line to see the book of Kells or to stretch your legs after a bus tour. You can stroll down to the Science Gallery, which is a part of Trinity College based on Pearse Street. Admission is free, and the Gallery shows a different exhibition every few months, cultivated by Irish scientists and focussing on technology, modern science and research, psychology and more.

33. HAVE YOUR FUNNY BONE TICKLED AT THE LAUGHTER LOUNGE

The Laughter Lounge is a great way to spend an evening. Based off O'Connell Street, the Laughter Lounge is Ireland's biggest comedy club. Tickets are usually inexpensive, and Irish comedians hit the stage every Thursday to Saturday. The lounge also regularly hosts charity nights throughout the year. Dubliners love a good laugh, so make sure to book your tickets online a couple of days in advance. The lounge also serves plenty of food and has a fully stocked bar, so you can eat, drink and laugh to your heart's content throughout the show. Within the venue, there is also the After Lounge, where you can have a dance after the sketches and bump elbows with fellow comedy lovers. The Laughter Lounge is hugely popular with work events, hen parties and stag groups so nights here can get a bit rowdy. The lounge is close to an abundance of good bars and nightclubs too, so it is the perfect place to start off your night out in Dublin.

34. CATCH A MUSICAL AT ONE OF DUBLIN'S FAMOUS THEATRES

Musicals have always captured the heart of the Irish public, and the modern day is no different. No matter what time of the year you plan to visit, you will always find a musical production to entertain you in one of Dublin's dedicated theatres. The Gaiety Theatre on South King Street opened in 1871 and hosts some of Ireland's most famous productions, including the world-renowned high energy Riverdance and the adored annual Christmas Pantomime. The Gaiety is well known among Dubliners for its drama and glamour. It also hosted the Eurovision song contest in 1971. The Bord Gais Energy Theatre (pronounced "board gosh") is another venue built to house some of Ireland's biggest musical productions, ranging from classical music concerts and ballet performances to the West-End and Broadway musicals. It is situated in Grand Canal on the south side of the Quays, easily accessible by DART. It is Ireland's largest fixed seat theatre and the building itself is eye-catchingly modern and dramatic in design. There are many more theatres in Dublin city, each hosting a wide range of musical productions. You will be humming show tunes for the rest of your trip!

35. VISIT THE HOME OF THE GAA

Like most cultures, sports play a huge part in Irish life. The GAA stands for Gaelic Athletic Association, which is the largest sporting organisation in Ireland. It oversees traditional Irish Gaelic football, hurling and camogie. GAA sports have captured the attention of international audiences their fast pace, demanding each GAA player to be athletic and highly skilled. Most Irish people will grow up playing one or more of these sports in school for their home clubs, therefore they continue to have a huge following today, especially in Dublin where the population is much higher than in other Irish counties. The city is home to the largest sports stadiums in Ireland, and tickets to spectate at GAA games are easily accessible. Croke Park is located on the north side of the city. "Croker", as it is more commonly known by locals, is the headquarters of the GAA and has been hosting coveted All-Ireland finals for generations. It is one of the largest stadiums in Europe and boasts 82,300 seats, as well as a modern GAA Museum where you can test your own hurling and Gaelic football skills. However, a trip to Croker would not be complete without sitting in the famous stands to watch a thrilling GAA match. You may not be lucky enough the secure tickets to an All-Ireland final, but there are many other events that you can secure tickets for using Ticketmaster or the Croke Park website. If there is a GAA match on you would like to watch, you don't need to make the trip to Croke Park. You can be sure that each pub in the city will be showing the match on screen, so kick back with a pint and enjoy the action with the pub's regulars. If the match you want to watch is not being shown on the screens, politely ask the bar staff to change for you - they are more than pleased to show off their national sport to interested tourists.

36. WATCH ONE OF THE IRELAND'S COMPETITIVE RUGBY TEAMS

Rugby is a very popular sport in Dublin. Ireland boasts four Pro14 rugby teams, as well as the successful Irish National Team, who compete in the Six Nations and the Rugby World Cup. There are several rugby stadiums in Dublin, including the Aviva Stadium (also known as Lansdowne Road) and the RDS Main Arena in Ballsbridge. Both stadiums are easy to get to from the city centre and draw large crowds on matchday. A ticket to a ruby match is very easy to source online using Ticketmaster. Depending on the type of match, it can be an inexpensive and enjoyable day out. Irish national team matches can be slightly more expensive, but very exciting to watch. If you are going to watch a match at any of Dublin's stadiums, I would recommend using public transport as the roads leading to the arena will be closed off to traffic and parking may be difficult to source. If watching a match on a colder day, make sure to wrap up in plenty of warm layers as the large stadiums can be quite chilly.

37. FOR SOCCER FANS, CATCH A BOHEMIANS FC MATCH AT DALYMOUNT PARK

The Irish Soccer League is not as popular as GAA sports and Irish soccer matches don't attract as large a crowd as at Irish rugby games. However, there are few sport events that evoke as much passion as local soccer matches in Dublin, described by some visitors as the best matchday experience in Ireland. Dalymount Park is an old-school football stadium tucked away in the north side suburb Phibsboro, the home of Bohemians Football Club, otherwise known as "Bohs". You can check the fixtures at Dalymount Park and purchase matchday tickets on the Bohemians FC website. A trip to Dalymount Park is very inexpensive, and hugely worthwhile. Bohs fans are notoriously passionate. Before you know it, you will be cheering and shouting along to some of their hilariously catchy matchday songs. Regardless of whether you are a die-hard soccer fan or a casual football spectator, a Bohs match is a once in a lifetime experience. Dalymount Park itself is a sports relic that has been around since 1901. Make sure to wear black and red to show your support for the home team. Be aware that away supporters are often just as animated as the Bohs crowd. Shouting expletives and insults across the field to the away crowd is very common for a Bohs match - and is all part of the fun!

38. FOR ALL NATURE LOVERS, VENTURE TO THE NATIONAL BOTANIC GARDENS OF IRELAND IN GLASNEVIN

Adjacent to the historic Glasnevin Cemetery is the immaculate Botanic Gardens, Ireland's scientific institution for botany and horticulture. The Gardens boast some of the world's most diverse and well-kept glasshouses, which are open all year round and completely free to the public. There are over three hundred endangered species of plants at the National Botanic Gardens, and six species that are already extinct in the wild. As conservation and science is the focus of the Garden, picnics and ball games are not allowed in the green areas. However, you are free to roam the stunning grounds for as long as you please. Springtime is especially stunning at the Botanic Gardens as the flowers begin to bloom. There is a garden tea-room open seven days a week, serving sweet treats and coffees. A visit to the Gardens is probably one of the most calming excursions you can take in the city, plus it is a great location for photos.

39. FOR FASHIONISTAS, DIVE INTO DUBLIN'S VINTAGE AESTHETIC

Over the past few years, Dublin's fashion trends have changed, largely influenced by a drive toward sustainability as opposed to fast fashion. Dublin's vintage clothes stores noticed a massive surge in popularity, many of whom are independent business owners. Vintage and pre-loved clothes are now celebrated among Dubliners. Dublin luckily has some of the best independent vintage clothes stores in Ireland, with quality one-of-a-kind stock that is both inexpensive and unique. Many of these vintage retailers are located conveniently in Temple Bar in the city centre. Nine Crows, Siopella (pronounced shop-ah-ella) and Tola Vintage are a few of the up-market vintage clothes retailers in Dublin. If you keep venturing south in the city, you will also find Om Diva on Drury Street and many small vintage clothes

kiosks located in George's Arcade. If you find
yourself in Bray village in Wicklow, pop into my
favourite vintage clothes shop, Finders Keepers.
Whether you are looking for a pair of vintage Levi
jeans or a second-hand jumper, you are bound to find
a unique treasure in one of the shops dotted around
the city to take home with you, much to the envy of
your pals.

Get some fresh air along one of Dublin's famous
walks

40. AMBLE ALONG THE COAST ON THE BRAY TO GREYSTONES WALK

As a county beside the Irish Sea, Dublin enjoys an
abundance of lovely coastal and cliff walks, each one
as beautiful as the other and completely free to enjoy.
One of the most popular walks among Dubliners is
the Bray to Greystones walk. The walk actually
begins and ends in County Wicklow, a county on the
border of Dublin that also shares the coastline.
However, it is super accessible from Dublin, as the
DART will bring you to Bray Train Station from

many of the stations in Dublin City. From there, you make your way along the promenade to the walking trail, which is signposted throughout the town. Bray is also a very popular village for Dubliners to venture to on sunny days for its many ice cream vendors and treat cafés, such as the famous Teddy's. The views here are gorgeous and the village is well worth a quick wander around before taking on the 7-kilometre walk, which is an easy trek along the cliffs facing the Irish Sea. Wear comfortable shoes, and if the sun is out don't forget your sun cream, as the coastal wind is prone to burning paler skin (as I have unfortunately learnt from experience). When you get to Greystones, another picturesque sea-side Wicklow town, make sure to take a trip to the famous Happy Pear café. This vegan café is hugely popular among Dubliners and is one of my favourite lunch spots. If the queue for the Happy Pear is too long, don't worry. Greystones is full of great cafés, restaurants and pubs to refresh yourself after your long walk. When you're ready to head back to the city, there is a DART station in Greystones that will bring you straight to back Dublin's city centre.

41. TAKE ON HOWTH HEAD

On the north side of the city is the coastal suburb of Howth, also served by a DART station and plenty of bus routes making it another super accessible walking location. The Howth Cliff Path Loop wraps around the peninsula Howth Head and is 6 to 10 kilometres long, depending on which path you take. This walk is one of my favourite trails in Dublin. The fresh air, greenery and sea views make it feel like you are miles from the city. Like the Bray to Greystones walk, make sure you are wearing some comfortable shoes. Ensure you don't stray too close to the edge of the cliff, especially if there is some wind. There are a couple of moderately difficult uphill trails to choose from if you feel like a challenge. However, if you would prefer to chat to your pals and take in the views at a leisurely pace, you are in the right place.

42. DO SOME DOG-WATCHING AT ST ANNE'S PARK IN CLONTARF

Like most cities, Dublin has some beautiful public parks. St Anne's Park in Clontarf is 240 acres of lush greenery, trees and rose gardens based on the north side facing the Irish Sea. On the weekends, there is a popular farmer's market, outdoor yoga classes and puppy training classes that attract hundreds of Dubliners. There's a quaint café called Olive's Room open all week long that is always bustling and a great spot for picking up a coffee to walk around the park with. The best part about St Anne's park is the ample opportunities for dog-watching! There is a puppy play pen and plenty of cavorting canines on the green that are always entertaining for dog-lovers to spectate. As there are many apartments around the St Anne's area, Dubliners take their furry friends to the park for their walks no matter what the season, so you won't be disappointed.

43. HAVE A PICNIC AT THE ICONIC ST STEPHEN'S GREEN

No trip to Dublin would be complete without a venture to St Stephen's Green, the central park at the top of Grafton Street. Like the majority of Dublin areas, the park itself is steeped in history. It was once occupied by a group of insurgents from the Irish Citizen Army during the 1916 Easter Rising, who tried to barricade themselves into the park using stolen vehicles and by digging makeshift trenches around the parameter. They were then shot at by the British Army, who were themselves positioned in the Shelbourne Hotel facing the park, which is still in use today. The park is now a welcome refuge from the bustle of Grafton Street and a great place for people-watching and coffee drinking. It is home to several memorials and sculptures that are worth checking out while you are wandering around the park. You might be lucky enough to catch a dance lesson in session on the bandstand on the south side of the main garden. Don't forget to bring some bread for the ducks.

44. TAKE IN GEORGIAN DUBLIN AROUND MERRION SQUARE

Merrion Square is another central Dublin parkland area and is just a short walk from St Stephen's Green. The Square is famous for its red-brick Georgian architecture. The area was first developed in 1762, and housed some of the most famous Dubliners, including writer Oscar Wilde, of whom there is a statue in the small grassy park, and poet W.B. Yeats. On Thursdays, park visitors can avail of a lunchtime market. There are also numerous artists displaying their pieces along the parameter of the park. There are pretty walkways and plenty of lawns to relax and have a picnic. The Georgian buildings have pleased the eyes of tourists and Dubliners for years. The old architecture, huge windows and famous colourful doors of Merrion Square are the subject of many international published works of art and photography, and even some Instagram pages, as walking around Merrion Square transports you back in time to Georgian Dublin.

45. VISIT THE NATURE RESERVE ON BULL ISLAND

Bull Island is an island in Dublin Bay that is only around 5 kilometres long and 800 metres wide. It is now a nature reserve and has the popular sandy beach called Dollymount Strand. It is easily accessible using Dublin Bus, which will leave you at Clontarf and you can then walk the wooden bridge to the island. If you're lucky, you might catch some seals in the waters or relaxing on the rocks, as the island is a seal breeding ground. There are also many different species of birds, rabbits, hares, foxes and other small mammals who call Bull Island home that you may catch a glimpse of. It is a popular walking and running location for Dubliners. The fresh sea air is invigorating at any time of the year. The views of Dublin Bay and Poolbeg Lighthouse are picturesque from the Island and offer a different perspective to Dublin than you will see from within the city centre. Clontarf village is also a scenic sea-side area of Dublin and worth a stroll.

46. GET UP CLOSE TO THE POOLBEG LIGHTHOUSE

The Poolbeg Lighthouse Walk, otherwise known as the Great South Wall Walk, is another lovely four-kilometre coastal walk that will take you out to the little red lighthouse that you can see from parts of Dublin Bay. You can get to the walk by getting the DART to Sandymount and walking from there. There are also a couple of Dublin bus routes that serve the area. It can be a bit cold and windy in this part of the county, so make sure you have a warm jacket and a pair of comfortable shoes. Rest assured, you will be delighted you made the trip. Poolbeg Lighthouse is a quaint little structure, and dates to 1768 when it was at first operated by candlelight! There are gorgeous views of the Bay in each direction from the top of the promenade and you can watch ships and trawlers coming in and out of the busy port for as long as you please.

47. TAKE A DIP AT THE FORTY FOOT

Even though Dublin is a coastal location, sea swimming is only popular among the toughest of Dubliners. This is because the sea around Dublin is FREEZING cold almost all year round. Many swimmers will wear wetsuits when taking on the bitter water. The Forty Foot in Dun Laoghaire (pronounced dun-leer-ee) is the most popular swimming spot in Dublin. Swimmers have been enjoying the Forty Foot for over 250 years. The area was immortalised in James Joyce's infamous novel Ulysses and lovers of the Irish writer all over the world have flocked here for generations. The entrance has a "Men Only" sign, but don't worry, that is a left-over relic from a by-gone era when only men were permitted to swim here. The sea water is deep and quite clean, however if you are hardy enough to take a dip, make sure to heed the warning signs that will alert you to any rocky areas that you need to avoid. The best way to get to the Forty Foot from the city is by taking the DART to Sandycove station and walking for ten to fifteen minutes. During the summer months the spot can be packed with revellers. If it is a sunny day, I would recommend venturing out early to avoid the crowds, whether you are going for a swim or simply watching the fun from the top with a warm drink. There is a changing area to get out of your swimsuits after your dip and the area is very well kept. The most popular day for the Forty Foot is surprisingly Christmas Day! Hundreds of Dubliners congregate at the Forty Foot for an icy Christmas morning plunge, a festive tradition that has been in place for as long as many Irish people can remember. I don't think you need any further proof that Dubliners are bit crazy!

48. TREK TO THE TOP OF DALKEY AND KILLINEY HILL

Another popular walk among Dubliners is the walkway to the top of Dalkey and Killiney Hill. The popularity is due to how easy it is to get to using the DART and the fantastic views from the hilltops. Hop off the DART at the Dalkey stop and follow the Sorrento Road to the vertical stone steps known as the Cat's Ladder. This walk is quite steep, so be prepared for your legs to get a bit tired. If the weather at the summit of Dalkey Hill is clear, you can see all the way to the Sugar Loaf Mountain and the Wicklow Mountains. You could also be lucky enough to see the mountains of Wales across the Irish Sea. Keep walking left along the coastline and you will get to Killiney Hill. You might catch some paragliders out for a sail and there is perfect weather at the top for flying kites. The path down from Killiney Hill will take you past the Druid's Chair pub, which is a lovely place for a pit stop and some refreshment before you take off down Vico Road. The stroll to the train station in Killiney through the gardens is as beautiful as the view from the top of the hill. This is the perfect walk to wrap up your trip to Dublin, where you can reflect (or walk off the remnants of a hangover) and stretch your legs, taking in the crisp sea air and Dublin's natural green landscape.

49. HOW TO GET THE BEST OUT OF DUBLIN'S PUBLIC TRANSPORT

Dublin is quite compact in comparison to other European capitals, which makes it super easy for Dubliners and tourists to get around. There is no metro as there is in many other cities, but there are plenty of other means of public transport to avail of, all reasonably priced, clean and reliable. When you arrive in Dublin, whether by plane or at any of the ports, pick up a Leap Visitor Card. These are stocked at most convenience stores nationwide, including at the airport and all the major bus and train stations. The Visitor Leap Card is valid for one, three or seven days depending on how much you pay and allows for unlimited travel after you use it for the first time. The Leap card saves you a great deal as opposed to paying cash fares on public transport during your stay, so keep it safe.

You may notice that the DART is mentioned quite often. The DART is the convenient rail network that runs through the city and beyond along the Dublin coastline. When using the DART, simply "tag-on" with your green Leap card (like you would use a contactless visa card) at any of the Leap card points. These points are usually at the entrance to the station, but otherwise will be sign-posted on the platform. If you are unsure, don't hesitate to ask someone for help at the station. There are ticket inspectors frequently on public transport in Dublin and you must show these inspectors that you have "tagged-on" using your Leap card. Anyone on public transport who has not paid for a ticket or used their Leap card is unfortunately fined, so make sure to tag-on before each journey. When you have arrived at your destination, you may need to "tag-off" at the exit of the station before you can leave.

Dublin also has the modern Luas, which is the Irish for speed, that you will see passing by you in the city centre. The Luas is the light rail network that criss-crosses through the streets. At peak times, the trams are quite busy as Dubliners are going to and from work. However, during the day the Luas is a comfortable and quick way to get around the city centre. You must tag-on at the Luas stop platform before getting on the tram. These tag-on points will be sign-posted, but you will also spot other passengers tagging-on before their journey in case you are unsure. The Luas is a great way to get around, but the final trams are around midnight so make sure you bear that in mind while you are revelling in Dublin's buzzing nightlife.

Dublin Bus is also an efficient and speedy way to get to all your adventures. As with the DART and Luas, you must tag-on at the entrance to the bus. There are two ways of doing this: You can let the bus driver know where you are getting off the bus and the driver will use your card to deduct your bus fare. However, with the Leap Visitor Card you have unlimited travel so I would recommend that you use the tag-on point located inside the bus on the right beside the entrance. Dublin Bus will keep going unless the driver knows that you are getting off at the next bus stop. As such, there are stop buttons throughout the bus that you will need to press to alert your driver that you are hopping off at the next stop. There are announcements throughout the journey to let you know what bus stop is next, so you don't need to worry about missing it. Once you hear your stop announced, hit the stop button and you are good to go and enjoy some more Dublin adventures. Don't forget that if you're waiting at a Dublin bus stop and see your bus coming, you need to put out your hand to let

the driver know you want to get on their bus.
Otherwise, the driver will keep going on their planned
route. If the bus is too full of passengers,
unfortunately the driver must keep going, but don't
worry. Dublin bus is very frequent, and you won't be
waiting long for the next one to come along to take
you to your destination.

50. TALK TO DUBLINERS – THEY ARE GREAT CRAIC!

No matter what city I visit, I always try to strike up
conversation with the locals. If you're like me, you
are in luck! Dubliners love to travel and we know
what it feels like to be a wandering tourist exploring
another city. The Dublin accent is notoriously
distinct, however as English is our first language,
chatting with Dubliners is easy. As a nation, we are
modern and tolerant of all global communities and
nationalities. Bar and restaurant staff are naturally
friendly and will happily stop to shoot the breeze if
they are not too busy serving. If you're looking for
more travel tips, don't be afraid to ask your waiter or
waitress if they have any suggestions. Dubliners are
very proud of their city and heritage and they will

gladly impart some wisdom or ask about your experiences so far on your visit. If you're in a pub, make small talk with the locals there. Let them know where you're from and see if they have advice on where to go and what to see to get the most out of your trip. Chat with some of your fellow Irish club-revellers on the dancefloor – they will know where else in Dublin to find a good time and might even invite you to join them on their escapades! On the street, if you need directions, you can politely approach passers-by or other passengers waiting for the bus. If you are respectful in your encounters, Dubliners will be pleasant in return. We love to share the city with tourists and hope that our visitors get the best craic out of Dublin city.

TOP REASONS TO BOOK THIS TRIP

First and foremost - the CRAIC!

The chance to learn about Irish heritage and history

Experiencing the beauty of Dublin's coastline

DID YOU KNOW?

The Irish for hello is dia duit (pronounced dee-ah gwit) and means "God to you". The response to this greeting is dia is Muire duit (dee-ah iss mwir-ah gwit) which means "God and Mary to you". You're guaranteed to get a big smile from any Dubliner for trying their native greeting.

Other greetings that Dubliners use daily and will serve you well throughout your trip are:

-    "What's the story?" (often shortened to just "story?" or "story, horse?")
-    "Are you well?" Often shortened to simply "well?"
-    "Sláinte!" (pronounced Slawn-tya) is the Irish salutation or version of "cheers!" – mainly heard in the pubs and bars

Dublin is the third smallest out of all 32 counties on the island, but over a third of Ireland's population live here.

There are over 750 licensed pubs in Dublin today – the oldest of which is The Brazen Head on Usher's Quay, a pub that dates all the way to 1198.

St Patrick's Day is celebrated all over the world as a tribute to the patron saint of Ireland, who is hailed in old stories as the man responsible for driving out all the snakes on the island. However, this is a myth, as there were never snakes in Ireland. He also did not wear a shamrock, nor did he wear green. He wasn't even Irish!

The Rotunda Maternity Hospital is the oldest maternity hospital in the world, dating back to 1745.

The first recorded open yacht race was held in Dublin Bay in 1663.

It is estimated that there are over 80 million people of Irish heritage living across the globe – which is 14 times more than the actual population of Ireland.

RESOURCES:

Viking Splash Tour:
    https://citysplashtours.com/Dublin

Guinness Storehouse: https://www.guinness-
    storehouse.com/en

1916 Rebellion Walking Tour:
    http://www.1916rising.com/

Ghost Bus Tour: https://ghostbus.ie/

Jameson Distillery:
    https://www.jamesonwhiskey.com/ie/visit-
    us/jameson-distillery-bow-st

Butlers Chocolate Factory:
    https://www.butlerschocolates.com/en/chocolate-
    experience/book-a-visit

Leprechaun Museum:
    http://www.leprechaunmuseum.ie/

National Print Museum:
    https://www.nationalprintmuseum.ie/

Irish Whiskey Museum:
https://www.irishwhiskeymuseum.ie/

EPIC The Irish Immigration Museum:
https://epicchq.com/

Kilmainham Gaol: http://kilmainhamgaolmuseum.ie/

Dublin Zoo: https://www.dublinzoo.ie/

Smock Alley Theatre: https://smockalley.com/

Irish Film Institute: https://ifi.ie/

Laughter Lounge: https://laughterlounge.com/

Gaiety Theatre: https://www.gaietytheatre.ie/

Bord Gais Energy Theatre:
https://bordgaisenergytheatre.ie/

Croke Park: https://crokepark.ie/

Bohemians FC/ Dalymount Park:
https://bohemianfc.com/

Leap Card information:
https://about.leapcard.ie/leap-visitor-card

Ticketmaster (for rugby fixtures and gigs):
https://www.ticketmaster.ie/

PACKING AND PLANNING TIPS

A Week before Leaving

- Arrange for someone to take care of pets and water plants.

- Email and Print important Documents.

- Get Visa and vaccines if needed.

- Check for travel warnings.

- Stop mail and newspaper.

- Notify Credit Card companies where you are going.

- Passports and photo identification is up to date.

- Pay bills.

- Copy important items and download travel Apps.

- Start collecting small bills for tips.

- Have post office hold mail while you are away.

- Check weather for the week.

- Car inspected, oil is changed, and tires have the correct pressure.

- Check airline luggage restrictions.

- Download Apps needed for your trip.

Right Before Leaving

- Contact bank and credit cards to tell them your location.

- Clean out refrigerator.

- Empty garbage cans.

- Lock windows.

- Make sure you have the proper identification with you.

- Bring cash for tips.

- Remember travel documents.

- Lock door behind you.

- Remember wallet.

- Unplug items in house and pack chargers.

- Change your thermostat settings.

- Charge electronics, and prepare camera memory cards.

READ OTHER
GREATER THAN A TOURIST
BOOKS

Greater Than a Tourist- Geneva Switzerland: 50 Travel Tips from a Local by Amalia Kartika

Greater Than a Tourist- St. Croix US Birgin Islands USA: 50 Travel Tips from a Local by Tracy Birdsall

Greater Than a Tourist- San Juan Puerto Rico: 50 Travel Tips from a Local by Melissa Tait

Greater Than a Tourist – Lake George Area New York USA: 50 Travel Tips from a Local by Janine Hirschklau

Greater Than a Tourist – Monterey California United States: 50 Travel Tips from a Local by Katie Begley

Greater Than a Tourist – Chanai Crete Greece: 50 Travel Tips from a Local by Dimitra Papagrigoraki

Greater Than a Tourist – The Garden Route Western Cape Province South Africa: 50 Travel Tips from a Local by Li-Anne McGregor van Aardt

Greater Than a Tourist – Sevilla Andalusia Spain: 50 Travel Tips from a Local by Gabi Gazon

Children's Book: *Charlie the Cavalier Travels the World* by Lisa Rusczyk Ed. D.

> TOURIST

Follow us on Instagram for beautiful travel images:

http://Instagram.com/GreaterThanATourist

Follow *Greater Than a Tourist* on Amazon.

>Tourist Podcast

>T Website

>T Youtube

>T Facebook

>T Goodreads

>T Amazon

>T Mailing List

>T Pinterest

>T Instagram

>T Twitter

>T SoundCloud

>T LinkedIn

>T Map

> TOURIST

At *Greater Than a Tourist,* we love to share travel tips with you. How did we do? What guidance do you have for how we can give you better advice for your next trip? Please send your feedback to GreaterThanaTourist@gmail.com as we continue to improve the series. We appreciate your constructive feedback. Thank you.

METRIC CONVERSIONS

TEMPERATURE

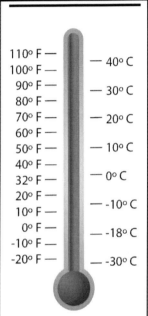

110° F — — 40° C
100° F —
90° F — — 30° C
80° F —
70° F — — 20° C
60° F —
50° F — — 10° C
40° F —
32° F — — 0° C
20° F —
10° F — — -10° C
0° F — — -18° C
-10° F —
-20° F — — -30° C

To convert F to C:

Subtract 32, and then multiply by 5/9 or .5555.

To Convert C to F:

Multiply by 1.8 and then add 32.

32F = 0C

LIQUID VOLUME

To Convert:...................Multiply by
U.S. Gallons to Liters................ 3.8
U.S. Liters to Gallons 26
Imperial Gallons to U.S. Gallons 1.2
Imperial Gallons to Liters........ 4.55
Liters to Imperial Gallons 22
1 Liter = .26 U.S. Gallon
1 U.S. Gallon = 3.8 Liters

DISTANCE

To convert ....Multiply by
Inches to Centimeters 2.54
Centimeters to Inches 39
Feet to Meters....................... .3
Meters to Feet 3.28
Yards to Meters 91
Meters to Yards 1.09
Miles to Kilometers 1.61
Kilometers to Miles............ .62
1 Mile = 1.6 km
1 km = .62 Miles

WEIGHT

1 Ounce = .28 Grams
1 Pound = .4555 Kilograms
1 Gram = .04 Ounce
1 Kilogram = 2.2 Pounds

TRAVEL QUESTIONS

- Do you bring presents home to family or friends after a vacation?

- Do you get motion sick?

- Do you have a favorite billboard?

- Do you know what to do if there is a flat tire?

- Do you like a sun roof open?

- Do you like to eat in the car?

- Do you like to wear sun glasses in the car?

- Do you like toppings on your ice cream?

- Do you use public bathrooms?

- Did you bring a cell phone and does it have power?

- Do you have a form of identification with you?

- Have you ever been pulled over by a cop?

- Have you ever given money to a stranger on a road trip?

- Have you ever taken a road trip with animals?

- Have you ever gone on a vacation alone?

- Have you ever run out of gas?

- If you could move to any place in the world, where would it be?

- If you could travel anywhere in the world, where would you travel?

- If you could travel in any vehicle, which one would it be?

- If you had three things to wish for from a magic genie, what would they be?

- If you have a driver's license, how many times did it take you to pass the test?

- What are you the most afraid of on vacation?

- What do you want to get away from the most when you are on vacation?

- What foods smell bad to you?

- What item do you bring on ever trip with you away from home?

- What makes you sleepy?

- What song would you love to hear on the radio when you're cruising on the highway?

- What travel job would you want the least?

- What will you miss most while you are away from home?

- What is something you always wanted to try?

- What is the best road side attraction that you ever saw?

- What is the farthest distance you ever biked?

- What is the farthest distance you ever walked?

- What is the weirdest thing you needed to buy while on vacation?

- What is your favorite candy?

- What is your favorite color car?

- What is your favorite family vacation?

- What is your favorite food?

- What is your favorite gas station drink or food?

- What is your favorite license plate design?

- What is your favorite restaurant?

- What is your favorite smell?

- What is your favorite song?

- What is your favorite sound that nature makes?

- What is your favorite thing to bring home from a vacation?

- What is your favorite vacation with friends?

- What is your favorite way to relax?

- Where is the farthest place you ever traveled in a car?

- Where is the farthest place you ever went North, South, East and West?

- Where is your favorite place in the world?

- Who is your favorite singer?

- Who taught you how to drive?

- Who will you miss the most while you are away?

- Who if the first person you will contact when you get to your destination?

- Who brought you on your first vacation?

- Who likes to travel the most in your life?

- Would you rather be hot or cold?

- Would you rather drive above, below, or at the speed limited?

- Would you rather drive on a highway or a back road?

- Would you rather go on a train or a boat?

- Would you rather go to the beach or the woods?

TRAVEL BUCKET LIST

1.

2.

3.

4.

5.

6.

7.

8.

9.

10.

NOTES

Made in United States
North Haven, CT
07 February 2025

65574603R00067